NOT A THROUGH STREET

NOT A THROUGH STREET

PETE OROZCO

LitPrime Solutions
21250 Hawthorne Blvd
Suite 500, Torrance, CA 90503
www.litprime.com
Phone: 1 (209) 788-3500

© 2021 Pete Orozco. All rights reserved.

No part of this book may be reproduced, stored in a retrieval system, or transmitted by any means without the written permission of the author.

Published by LitPrime Solutions   03/04/2021

ISBN: 978-1-954886-27-8(sc)
ISBN: 978-1-954886-28-5(e)

Library of Congress Control Number: 2021904893

Any people depicted in stock imagery provided by iStock are models, and such images are being used for illustrative purposes only.

Certain stock imagery © iStock.

Because of the dynamic nature of the Internet, any web addresses or links contained in this book may have changed since publication and may no longer be valid. The views expressed in this work are solely those of the author and do not necessarily reflect the views of the publisher, and the publisher hereby disclaims any responsibility for them.

CONTENTS

Dedication vii

La Shorty and Jesse. 1
Carlos 4
Andrew. 7
Ledell, Veronica and John. 10
Bobby 15
Sonia. 18
Muchisky 21
Three Lovable Characters. 24
Shelly 28
Tony 30
Marianne 32
Paul. 35
Phil Catalano and Bill Putman. 39
Rudy. 44
C- School Softball 46
The Black Widow. 48
Bam Bam 50
Pancho Villa 55
Graduation Day 57
The Haunted House. 61
The Penny Carnival 63
Loni 65

Coach John Wooden 67
Show Business Teacher 69
Maricruz 71
The Classroom Computer Man 73
The Bongo Woman 76
Sister Aurora 78
King Tut 82
Smooth 83
The Piruvians 85
Conclusion 86

DEDICATION

BY PETE OROZCO

The year was 1971. I was tired of working at boring, low paying, no future jobs. I made the decision that I wanted to become a classroom teacher. In making that decision, I realized that I had to go back to college and earn a degree. I also understood that I would have to complete a teacher training program in order to earn a teaching certificate. At that time finding a teaching position was extremely difficult but everyone assured me that would improve. Sure enough, it did and I found myself working pretty regularly as a substitute teacher in junior high schools and high schools in Oxnard, California. Unfortunately, every school year found me employed at a different school accompanied by promises that full time employment would soon follow but each August I found that the position that I was counting on had been cut for financial reasons. That meant that I had to apply to different school districts in Ventura County in search of a position. I was for that reason that I found myself in the school administration office at Fillmore, California in August of 1982. I had applied for a teaching position at the alternative school there call Fillmore Community High School. At the interview that day I met the interview committee which consisted of the Principal, Secretary and the lone teacher Owen Muchisky. Owen was a long-time Special

Education teacher who had chosen to work at the alternative high school. As Owen later told me, the moment that I came into the room, he knew that he wanted to work with me in a team-teacher relationship. Of all the things that I expected to need in order to become a successful teacher, the one that I had not counted on was a mentor. Owen became that mentor and over the next twenty-five years we worked together as a perfect team. The characteristics that each of us brought to the table merged into a hugely successful team. Due to his experience and background, I followed his lead and learned something new nearly every day. Over the years, we became close friends, bought property to share our homes on and he was the best man when I married Sylvia in 1989. At one point, years later he asked me to be responsible for his daughter Deana if anything should happen to him and his wife Birdie. Our families traveled together and we attended sporting events all over California. When he retired, I told him at the party we held to honor his career that I had always thought of him as the older brother I never had. At that point, I felt confident enough in my development to replace him as the lead teacher at the school. It was my turn to bring in a new teacher and work with him, or her to keep the atmosphere at the school fruitful. After he left Community high school, former students would stop by and ask about him. Even today, I am in contact with dozens of "C" school products on Facebook. They always ask, "How's Muchisky doing?" Owen died this past Christmas and numerous people replied to his obituary with kind words and memories. Over the last couple of years I talked to Owen concerning this book about our experiences and the characters we encountered. Now that I am finishing this project, my thoughts are once again with him. "Thanks brother."

LA SHORTY AND JESSE

It was a beautiful summer day, one of those Southern California summer days that made the place famous and enticed people from all over the world want to come live there. Two teenagers were walking down the street on their way to the local market. They were out to buy some breakfast, Funyuns, snickers bars and a soda to be exact. The girl, known to all her friends as La Shorty and her friend Jesse had known each other all their lives. They were not related or dating, they were just good friends. La Shorty was extremely short in stature, less than five feet tall. Not only did that explain her nickname, it also helped to explain her feisty attitude. She was often heard to say that she wasn't afraid of anyone, boys, girls, adults, even the police didn't intimidate her at all. More than once she told me how good it felt when someone was intimidated by her. "I love it when they're afraid" she said. La Shorty was very bright and could be quite personable when she wasn't feeling threatened. Her problems in school stemmed from the fact that this brightness rarely exhibited itself in the classroom. Perhaps the only time she felt a positive self-worth was when she got into a fight with someone, win or lose. Over the years that she was in my classroom, she told me of her terrible homelife. Her mother and father had split-up when she was quite young and her home had turned into the local party house for her mother's "friends". La Shorty was constantly suspended from school for fighting and being verbally abusive to teachers and staff at every school she had attended. She therefore fell further and further behind academically. By the time she landed at the alternative school where I worked, her reading and math skills were two or three years behind where she should have been. When she was finally able to learn how to control her emotions, telling me once, "I have to just swallow my anger", she quite easily caught up with her schoolwork. It is my firm belief that the structure and close supervision by the staff at our school was perfect for her needs. Jesse, on the other hand, just did not possess the natural intelligence to keep up in school. He rarely got into trouble for fighting at school. I never heard of nor witnessed Jesse being verbally abusive of anyone, students nor staff members. Because of this lower academic ability, he just did not see a need to attend school, at all. It was obvious that the classroom was not a comfortable place for him. Since kindergarten, Jesse had been absent from school nearly seventy-five percent of the time. This would usually result in his parents being called in to school where they chastised him in the presence of school administrators followed by his parents promising that he would not miss any more school days. A pattern developed that a few days later he ditched school again and he was therefore suspended from the high school, which is exactly what he wanted. By the time he arrived at the alternative high school, his parents, former teachers and administrators had all given-up hope for him. The reports that I read speculated that Jesse was just lazy. That may have been the case but also Jesse might have been better suited for Special Education. Unfortunately, he had missed so much school that it was impossible to assess him and qualify him for the Special Education classes that he needed. So, on this fine summer's day, as La Shorty and Jesse walked down the street, life was, in their minds all good. They talked about friends, getting loaded and upcoming parties, but mostly they talked about not having to go to school for another two months. As they walked, Jesse said, "Look, a bunch of pussies live on that street." La Shorty answered, "What do you mean?" Jesse then said, "The sign says Not a Tough Street!" La Shorty told me later, "Jesse's so stupid. The sign said Not a Through Street". She then began to laugh and shook her head from side to side. This story is so indicative of so many of the hundreds of students that I worked with over my thirty-year teaching career. So often they were so close to truly comprehending the world around them. And yet, they were not even close.

CARLOS

There was a new student that came to our school, his name was Carlos. Carlos was sixteen and an average looking young man. He had a quick, bright, inquisitive look about him making him appear to be capable of being successful in school. His past academic record indicated that for several years, he had been able to just get by in his classes. The record also showed a history of getting into numerous fights going back to his being in the third grade. Typically, a new student coming to our school took a few days to become adjusted to the surroundings, although they were almost always well acquainted with the other students and some of the staff. Our alternative high school was quite different from any other school in the county, perhaps even the state. Students were expected to be in school every day, on time and work individually for at least four hours. Our school motto was, "We are firm, fair and consistent". Most students who came there had a long history of struggling in a comprehensive high school even before. Most of them usually became comfortable and accepted their situation, they bought into our structured environment. Many became successful, made progress academically and either returned to the traditional program to graduate or earned their high school diploma at our school. On the third day that Carlos was enrolled at our school, a fight broke out between two young men. Fighting was rare at our school but it did happen on occasion. The fact is that teenage boys (and to a lesser extent teenage girls) sometimes have a difficult time controlling their anger. Many of them can be extremely fragile and easily offended. When such an event took place, the staff (my co-teacher Owen Muchisky, the administrator, sometimes the secretary and myself) always stepped in, separated the combatants, usually allowing them to cool off and called their parents to take them home for the day. If the fight was exceptionally violent, both students would receive a two-day suspension. Very seldom did these types of events cause more than one intervention. The issue was usually resolved and everybody just moved on. After the school day came to an end, Owen and I went to lunch and discussed the disruption. He began to tell me something that he observed that I had not. Owen had a lot more experience than I in the teaching field. He had also worked with "At Risk" students for several years, I was in my fourth- year teaching and this was only the second time that I had worked with such students. As we discussed the fight and our role in putting an end to it, Owen mentioned, "Did you see the look on Carlos' face during the fight". I admitted that I had not, that I was concentrating on the actual combatants. And Carlos had not become involved in the fight. He then told me that Carlos was pacing and panting as the boys fought. He then said, "the kid had an expression on his face during the fight that reminded him of documentaries that he had seen of wolves ready to jump in on a kill. His eyes were wide and wild. His body appeared to be shaking un-controllably, it seemed that it was all he could do to keep from jumping in to tear into either or both of the fighters." We decided to keep an eye on Carlos even though he had not done anything for which he needed to face discipline. Carlos remained a student at our school for the rest of the school year. He never caused any problems at school but a few months after the fight, he began to make a habit of faking a punch aimed at me every time we passed each other in the hallway. He never actually hit me but several times he came pretty close, holding back his punch just in time. Now Carlos was only about

5'6" and weighed about 140 pounds but I was becoming concerned that his not-so-playful punches might actually make contact with me. After a couple of weeks, I decided to inform our Principal of my concerns. He set up a meeting with Carlos and me in his office. The Principal hoped that by discussing my concerns, problems might be averted. He asked Carlos directly, "Have you been throwing punches at Mr. O.?" Carlos quickly answered, "I was just kidding him". "It didn't mean anything." The Principal then said, "Are you trying to fight with Mr. O.? He might think the wrong thing and actually punch you." Carlos then answered quickly directly at me "Go for it!" I then said, "I don't want to hurt you, son." The meeting ended, the Principal took no disciplinary action, there was no need to. Carlos was able to control his emotions for the rest of the term. He stopped faking punches directed at me and he never got into any fights at school. We did notice that a few weeks after the meeting, Carlos started spend a lot of his time with one of our female students. His attitude mellowed noticeably. Carlos finished the school year and since he had turned eighteen, decided to not return to school the next semester. I would occasionally see Carlos around town. He never demonstrated any anger toward me. I heard that he and the girl from our school had a baby together. He apparently found a job and was able to settle into an acceptable life.

ANDREW

His name was Andrew Fayloga. I was working at a junior high school in Oxnard, CA. One morning when I arrived at school, I was met in by the Principal. He called me into his office where he told me that I would be acquiring a new student that day. The student's name was Andrew Fayloga and his was a special case. The Principal proceeded to tell me that Andrew was a typical 7th grade student with one major difference, he was dying. He had brain cancer and I was told that he probably would not live through the semester. His family had requested that no special accommodation be made for him. They just wanted him to feel like he was any other thirteen-year old. When Andrew arrived at my classroom that morning, he appeared extremely frail with dark circles around his eyes. He did not say much of anything that first day, I had decided to simply introduce him as a new student to the rest of the class as he sat in his seat. As it turned out, I didn't have to be concerned about how the class accepted him, they all knew about his situation and that Andrew would not be a part of our class for very long. A few weeks went by and Andrew seemed to be doing alright under the circumstances, at least he wasn't showing signs of deteriorating. One afternoon, as I stood in the hallway supervising students moving between classrooms, one of the female student coming to my classroom ran up to me excitedly. She said, "Billy was chasing someone and accidently bumped into Andrew. He knocked him to the ground." I knew Billy, he was the biggest student at the school. He was usually very gentle, conscious of his size and was careful around the girls and smaller students. Apparently when he knocked Andrew down, all of the students around him froze and gasped. The students were all very gentle around him and this accident really scared them. Andy felt very bad but everything turned out well, Andrew wasn't injured in the least. Things returned to normal around the school. Most days, Andrew didn't seem to be suffering or in pain. As we approached the end of the Fall semester, I was hopeful that the students wouldn't have to experience more trauma concerning Andrew. Then, with about a week to go in the semester, Andrew missed several days of school. This was unusual, his attendance had been very regular up until then. Finally, on a Friday afternoon, I received a message from the office that Andrew had died. I was told to make the announcement to the students in my classroom. They were all very quiet. No one appeared to get overly emotional. They all seemed to have accepted his death as inevitable. For most of them, this was the first time that anyone they knew had died. Some had lost a family member but this was a young person that they had grown to accept, protect and admire. In those days, the schools did not provide any type of grief counseling as is so common now. It was also my first experience dealing with the death of someone so young. I was still very new to teaching and it was difficult for me to truly comprehend the death of someone who was just starting out on his life journey. A few days afterward, I saw the obituary that was posted in the local newspaper. I decided there and then that I would put in an appearance at the visitation that was to be held at a local mortuary. Not knowing how to deal with this, I nearly backed out on going that Saturday afternoon. When I did arrive, I saw the Fayloga family in the small viewing room. I had met Andrew's mother when he first enrolled in our school so I walked up to the her and introduced myself to her and Andrew's father as one of Andrew's teachers. Mrs. Fayloga's eyes were slightly red but otherwise she seemed very calm. She just seemed to have accepted all of this a long time ago. Andrew's father seemed a little surprised that I was there at all. Eventually he shook my hand and thanked me for coming. Also, in the room were two small children, a couple of years younger than Andrew. One of them walked up to the open casket and kissed Andrew on the forehead. As I stood there, I noticed that the family had put several of Andrew's favorite toys, stuffed animals, cars and toy soldiers, in the casket with Andrew. I didn't see anyone actually crying in the room. It all appeared to be a family just saying good-bye to their young loved one. Unfortunately, Andrew wasn't the only student that died while in one of my classes.

LEDELL, VERONICA AND JOHN

When you choose to become a teacher, you to look forward to having the opportunity to work with young people at the beginning of their lives with all their energy and enthusiasm. Many days I would wake up in the morning telling myself, "I get to go to work". You have an opportunity to ride the tide of the student's emotions. You never really know what is going to happen as each day at school begins. I used to think back how it was when I was their age. Back then, I had such excitement just thinking about my future and so many questions about where my journey would take me. I was thirty-four years old when I finally began my full-time teaching career and although the times were so different for high school students at that time than they had been for me, we shared a common belief that life would be interesting, fun and challenging and last for many, many years. As I mentioned earlier, a student named Andrew Fayloga from one of my classes died at age fourteen. It was sad and devasting for his family as well as difficult for the students who knew him. But Andrew had been ill for some time. Everyone knew that his time on earth was limited to a few months. We all had time to prepare for his death. This somehow seemed to ease the pain and sadness for everyone. Several years later, death again came knocking at our classroom door. No one was ready this time. Over less than a month, we had three students ripped out of our classroom. The staff and the forty students were emotionally sent reeling. The first student was named Ledell. He was a tall, dark-skinned young man who had only been enrolled in our little school for a couple of months. Ledell, had a very quick and agile mind. School work was not difficult for him and his bright personality made him extremely popular with most of the students. He had some athletic ability and probably would have been a successful athlete at most high schools except for one major detriment, he was one of the most rebellious, anti-authority figure young people that I had ever encountered. His behavior had gotten him removed from the traditional high school and when he came to our alternative high school, he carried his anger at the world over to our staff. Many students came to our school with these damaging emotions but they usually found a way to deal with it and became successful. As I say, he was extremely popular with the students in our school so when he was elected ASB President a few weeks after arriving, he seemed to be making some positive adjustments. I have found it amazing over my life how a little success in some area can improve someone's outlook at the world. In those days at our school, ASB Officers planned activities and operated the Snack Shop on campus. They sold sodas, chips and candy during the breaks to raise money for field trips and sports equipment that the students used throughout the school year. In doing so, ASB Officers were also in charge of making bank deposits and managing the bank account under the staff's supervision. The four ASB Officers would, on a rotating basis, take cash from the sales in the snack bar to the bank and return with a deposit slip which they then handed over to our secretary. We had done this for several years and had never encountered a problem. The program gave the ASB Officers some practical experience in responsibility as well as a certain elevated status among the students. One Friday afternoon, Owen, as ASB Advisor and our secretary had a meeting about the bank account.

Afterward, Owen came into my classroom. The students had left the campus at the end of the school day. As he came into my classroom, I had never seen him so angry. He and the secretary had discovered that quite a bit of money was missing from the bank account. They traced it back and found that several of the deposits that Ledell had made were short. He had been stealing money for several weeks. The Principal got involved at that point and together with Owen, they made plans to confront Ledell on Monday morning. They never got the chance. That night, being a Friday, nearly all of the students at both the traditional high school as well as our alternative high school gathered for parties all over the valley. Ledell was riding in a car going out to pick up another of our students, Veronica Herrera, at her house about eight miles from town. As they drove back into town, there was a head-on collision with another car. Both Ledell and Veronica were killed instantly. In a city with a bigger population and a school with larger enrollment, the impact might have been much different. At that time the town had a population of less than 15,000 and our school's enrollment was forty. Losing two extremely popular students in a flash of a second just devastated everyone at our school, both staff and students. Veronica was even more popular than Ledell. She was pretty, friendly and everything a seventeen girl should be. The reason that she had been sent to our school wasn't that she had been a problem for the high school staff, she just wasn't very motivated to complete her school-work or to even come to school regularly. Many of the girls who came to our school shared this damaging characteristic. They just didn't see how earning a high school diploma was all that important. Veronica focused her attention on her hair, make-up and clothes. She just knew that she would find a nice guy, settle down with him and have children, some day. In the meantime, life was meant for having fun. No one, especially Veronica, thought that her life would end that night. When school opened again on Monday, the entire population, both students and staff was as sad and depressed as any group of people that I had ever seen. This included Owen and myself, as well as the Principal and our secretary. It didn't seem possible that these young, fun loving, vital people were gone. We had a part time counselor who came in regularly to hold group meetings where the students discussed their issues and concerns. The Principal called the counselor and he came in to hold a session that included all of the students and staff. Tears flowed throughout the morning. I was very impressed how the counselor was able to model grief for the students. He was able to show the students that tears and sadness were appropriate. Grief is a very difficult emotion to deal with anytime. Even with the challenges that Ledell provided, nobody was prepared to deal with such a sudden end for two such well-liked young people.

As difficult as this was for the students, it was even more devastating for my teaching partner Owen. The anger that he had felt about what Ledell had done, stealing the ASB funds, made Owen even more conflicted. He and the Principal had been prepared to confront and potentially expel Ledell from school on Monday morning. When Owen heard the news Saturday morning about the car crash and the deaths of Ledell and Veronica he was even more angry and frustrated. Death makes you change how you feel about life in general. In this case, the deaths of two young people caused tremendous pain for the adults at the school. It just was not right for young people to die at such a young age, even for one who had committed such a terrible act. Owen had trusted Ledell with money and Ledell had let him down. Owen took this very personally. When Ledell died that night, Owen just didn't know how to react. It took him a long time to accept what had happened.

School was dismissed the day of the funerals. Everyone involved in the school attended the funerals. The entire staff, including the part-time counselor, worked very hard to ease the students back into the routine nature of our school. These efforts seemed to help the students move on from the loss of their friends. I believe that again, the structure and consistency that we provided for the students helped a lot. I am convinced that most young people actually crave and enjoy this supportive atmosphere. For many of our students, that was exactly what was missing in their homes. Over the years, the staff recognized that nearly 70% of our students did not live at home with their parents. Many lived with relatives, some with friends families and many of our female students lived in the homes of their boyfriends.

About three weeks after the crash that killed Ledell and Veronica, another student was killed one weekend while riding his motorcycle. His name was John Stroh. John was a likable, short in stature Caucasian kid. He had been enrolled in our school only a few weeks and he seemed to get along with just about everyone at our school, even the staff. John was usually in the company of a group that we usually called "The Stoners" and while I had no actual knowledge that he used marijuana regularly, it was well known that most of the kids that he was with did. This group was usually small in numbers, the true minority at our school. Their preferred type of music was what we used to call "Heavy Metal". The students in this group were also not very motivated academically. For the most part, they attended school fairly regularly and stayed out of trouble. When John died, the students didn't seem to take it as hard as they did the previous deaths. It did have the effect of compounding the depression that permeated the school for the remainder of the school year.

BOBBY

In addition to my job as a classroom teacher, I also enjoyed coaching sports teams wherever I was working. Early in my career, I had volunteered to coach teams at two other schools, one while teaching there and another as only a basketball coach. At the first school, the Principal had put out a notice that basketball coaches were needed and I applied. I was told that the A and B teams already had coaches but that a coach for the C team was open. The C team was made up of the smallest players on campus. There was no pay for this position but I really wanted to contribute. The first day of practice, sixteen boys turned out. The school was located in a mostly low income, minority area of town so most of the players were African-American or Mexican-American. On this day, there were also two Caucasian kids, Alan and Bobby. My coaching style was always the same. I demanded that the team play together at all times, that they always performed in a very disciplined manner, always under control. Each player had a particular role in contributing to the team's success. Those players who handled the ball well did their job putting the ball in a position for the team to score, those that were good a rebounding, did their job getting the ball after the opponent shot and missed or keeping it in play when one of their teammates missed a shot.

The players who shot the ball well were counted on to score points. Some players were better at playing defense, the most important job of all. One of my mottos was, "We can't win the game if we don't stop the other team from scoring". This did not mean that players who played defense were not allowed to shoot the ball, it just meant that their priority job was to play defense. Also, those who shot well were also required to play defense. It was a team game consisting of many individual skills. After a couple of practices, it became obvious that I had identified several good ball handlers and a few good rebounders. I also recognized some excellent good defensive players. Defensive players are made, not born, it took a lot of work on their part. Defensive players have to have the ability to make a commitment to the team to focus on their job, keeping the opponents from scoring <u>as few points as possible.</u> At that point in the developing season, I had not recognized a good, consistent shooter. Shooters are usually the direct opposite of defensive players. Shooters possess must possess tremendous confidence in themselves. They need to be just short of arrogant. Shooters expect every shot that they put up to go in the basket. If they happen to miss a couple of shots, their self-confidence convinces them that they just need to keep on shooting. Eventually, the ball will rip the net. On the fourth day of practice, I found my shooter. His name was Bobby. Bobby had a Hispanic last name but didn't look Hispanic. He had very light-colored skin, straight blond hair and blue eyes. I found out later that he had been adopted as an infant. He was raised by a Hispanic family and grew up in The Barrio. When he talked, he sounded just like the rest of the Hispanic students and players. In his mind, he wasn't white, he was a Homeboy. Shooting a basketball successfully and repeatedly requires balance, starting with the feet and moving up through the body with a rhythmic motion that culminates with a flick of the wrist with the pointing finger of the shooting pointing at the basket. Some players work on this for years, most never attain the knack. Bobby had somehow learned how to do this all on his own. My job as the coach was to then develop an offensive scheme for this team that began with the point guard handling the ball successfully down the court. He then made a quick, sharp pass to the player on the right wing (Bobby in this case). At that same moment, the player from the right baseline ran up and set a screen on the player guarding Bobby. Bobby took two or three dribbles to his right and put up about a 15 to 18 foot jump shot. The point guard stayed back to play defense and players on the left wing and left baseline moved toward the basket to rebound in case Billy missed. He rarely did. One day at practice, I was reviewing with the players our various strengths and areas that we needed to improve upon. As I ended my evaluation, I said, "And as far as shooting, we have the best shooter in Ventura County." Bobby's face just beamed. The players on the team accepted their roles and we had a great deal of success. I left the school the next year and moved on to another school. I never heard anything from or about Bobby. Perhaps his moment had passed. At least for those bright, shining moments in his life, Bobby was a success.

SONIA

In August of 1982, I was hired to work as a classroom teacher at an alternative school, a continuation high school. The school was in its third year of existence and was in the process of moving into new, portable buildings on the far edge of the local comprehensive high school campus. At that time, Continuation high schools had been around in California for about twenty years. Nearly every school district found it attractive to establish a continuation high school in order to meet the needs of students who found attending the comprehensive high school too difficult or challenging. The schools gave the students an extra chance to continue their education and even accelerate their completion of schoolwork toward a diploma. In addition, the motivation for the school district was to receive money from the state to replace monies lost by poor student attendance at the traditional high school. Continuation high schools also gave high school administrators an alternative placement for troubled students or girls preparing to have a baby. On my first day at this school, the Principal had set-up interviews with each new or returning student in order to meet the staff (One Principal, two classroom teachers and one secretary). As the portable classrooms were being assembled, the staff met with the students in a park immediately adjacent to the classroom buildings. I was just getting to know my fellow staff members and learning how the school would be run. It was a Thursday and school was scheduled to begin on Monday. We had met with about five students in brief meetings to introduce ourselves and establish what would be expected of each student. We were scheduled to meet with a returning student named Nancy. Nancy had attended the school sporadically during the previous semester. According to the Principal and secretary, she had been extremely uncooperative and even belligerent during her time there. She was seventeen years old and felt that she had gone to school long enough, she wanted to drop out. The other student was a fifteen year-old named Sonia. The staff knew very little about her except that she had failed all of her classes at the comprehensive high during the previous school year, her Freshman year. Nancy had a scheduled appointment to see us, Sonia was scheduled to meet with us later in the day. The thing that I will always remember was the look of complete and utter hatred on each of their faces that as they walked up to us on that afternoon. I had never personally seen either of the two young ladies before but they had already made the decision that we, they staff, were their mortal enemies. Something told me that it was going to be extremely difficult to reach these two. The school year began and after a few weeks, Nancy continued her typical pattern and just stopped attending school, again. She eventually referred to a County school program and refused to attend that school as well. My teaching partner, Owen Muchisky told me one day, "You can't reach them all." Sonia was a different story. She was younger and brighter. She was the eldest child of two very religious parents. Her father had been an outstanding athlete during his days in high school in our community and was currently working as a pastor in his church. Her mother didn't speak much English but it was obvious that Sonia really didn't want to disappoint either of her parents. It wasn't long before Sonia fell in line with our expectations. She rarely missed a day of school, applied herself to the subject matter that we assigned to her and her attitude that was so negative that first day, really began to soften. We could see that down deep inside, she wanted to please the staff and earn our respect and acceptance. One morning, as the students were on a break, I heard several voices coming from the boy's restroom. As the staff did regularly, I went into the restroom to make certain nothing inappropriate was taking place. I found four boys in the restroom and one girl, Sonia. I had several options available to me at that moment. I could have made a fuss, yelling and clearing the room, I could have singled out Sonia for being there in the first place and I could have kicked everyone out and locked the door. For some reason, I chose to just stand there in the corner of the restroom which had the effect of making all of the students very uncomfortable. No one said a word and they soon left the restroom. After that, Sonia seemed to tone down her rebelliousness and she slowly began to become successful in school. Her attendance became almost perfect and after four years, she did not have enough credits to graduate and the enrollment of the school was full, she had to leave. I remember she pulled me aside on her final day with us. She said, "I don't want to leave". I told her that it was time and that I knew she would succeed in whatever she attempted. We have remained friends to this day. She gave birth to a son and he has been a fine example to the entire community, an organizer of community events. Sonia worked at a series of, low paying, unfulfilling jobs before going back to school and earning a degree in computer science. At last report, she had found a job with the county as computer support worker. Those academic abilities that had been so buried in her early high school days had somehow surfaced and she was able to put them to good use. She has also become involved in a car club, traveling around the country showing her custom cars. Recently she sent me a posting of a Facebook article declaring that she had been selected for the Custom Car Hall of Fame, a national organization. I am still very proud of her.

MUCHISKY

Over my thirty years teaching, I met and observed hundreds of teachers at work in the schools. Some were very effective, enthusiastically interacting with students every minute of every day. They gave the appearance of loving their chosen profession and the students usually responded by joining in and making learning fun. Perhaps it was to be expected but these teachers also operated in a structured environment. The students understood and accepted this. They realized that some structure in the classroom would lead to their success. I like to believe that they took this knowledge out into the world as adults. There were a few teachers who once possessed this joy, but the years had begun to take a toll on their spirit. They seemed to be counting the days until they could retire and begin to enjoy life once again. For these teachers, their sentence was up. There were also a very few classroom teachers who should have never gotten into teaching in the first place. These sad, lonely people usually appeared to have been enthusiastic, successful students as students, loving school when they were young. It was obvious to me that they expected today's young people to bring the same excitement to school that these teachers had, never recognizing that some things in our society had changed. Their unrealistic expectations made it nearly impossible to reach the students in their classrooms. Thankfully for everyone involved, these teachers usually did not survive more than a couple of years in the classroom. Many of them moved on to other careers. Perhaps predictably, several of them became school administrators. Their attempts to extricate themselves from the stress and responsibility of the classroom only perpetuated their incompetence. On the other hand, the most successful classroom teacher that I ever witnessed in action has become my life-long mentor, partner and friend. The first time that I met Owen Muchisky, it was though we had known each other our entire lives. Owen was born in Detroit, Michigan but his mother and father moved to Corona, California when he was an infant. Growing up in the barrio of Corona, Owen had taken on many of the characteristics of the local homeboys. His best friends as a child and adolescence were Mexican-Americans from whom he learned just enough "street Spanish" to communicate with his neighbors and school mates. This up-brining came in quite handy in working with the population that attended the alternative school where we worked. He understood the world in which our students grew up, unlike most of the teachers and administrators at the traditional schools. This greatly helped me in my education and development as a teacher. Although my last name is Hispanic, I was raised in a white middle-class world. My father spoke Spanish but was taught as a child to use only English at home and school even though his mother spoke only Spanish. By the time my generation came along, we experienced so little Spanish that it was a lost language to me and my siblings. More importantly, whereas my values reflected the majority of Americans, Owen taught me, mostly by observation and example, how to approach minority students, particularly Mexican-Americans, and their parents on a level that stressed respect and communication. Time and again, over the years, I observed Owen as he was able to connect with a new minority student (majority at our school) who came to our school. The traditional atmosphere of confrontation between white teachers and dark-skinned students usually evaporated after a few days in our classrooms. Additionally, Owen was very talented in the methods he used to teach arithmetic and basic math skills. This was my weakest area to teach. I was more comfortable teaching English, Social Studies and Science. The single most common characteristic of the students that we worked with was that they had missed a lot of school days for several years. The result of this was that their basic skills in math, reading and writing were far behind where they should have been by that time. We found that by getting the students to come to school consistently, they usually made great progress in catching-up to where they should have been. Perhaps they were able to just sit at their desks and absorb and education. That was the key. Most of the students had the ability to complete coursework once they felt comfortable in an atmosphere of structure and consistent discipline. We found that nearly all of our students regardless of ethnicity, gender, culture or economic status wanted to be successful in school and make progress toward earning a high school diploma. They all wanted to please their parents and in order to do this, they realized that they needed to please their teachers and other staff members. Owen Muchisky was an advocate for young people who wanted to make something of themselves. I quickly became a disciple of his attitude and methods. In the twenty-five years that we worked together, as different as our personalities were, we were able to learn from each other and combine our skills to produce successful students. For several years we attended the Conventions of the California Continuation Education Association. When we introduced ourselves to other attendees we would always say, "We have been together longer than most married couples". We made a good team.

THREE LOVABLE CHARACTERS

Over the years, there was a great variety of student characters that found their way into my classrooms. As I mentioned previously, some were angry and bitter, tired of being treated like farm animals, herded from one school or classroom or teacher just to get rid of them. Many of our students came from families that had never seen a member graduate from high school. Often parents told their children that finding a job and being a hard-working person meant more that getting an education. Some students were so damaged by using marijuana and alcohol too often or abused by uncaring and too busy parents. We had girls come to our school after having given birth at age 14, 15 or 16. These girls often had such low self-esteem because of the manner in which their parents, society or educators looked down on them. I remember one girl telling me that it didn't matter to her if she graduated from high school or not. She said, "my homeboy will take care of me!" I saw her years later and she told me that she had four children by four different men, never marrying any of them. Another said once, "I don't need an education or even a job. I can receive enough money from welfare to take care of me and my baby". A quick glance at the "Permanent Records" of most of the students that I worked with indicated that they had a history of poor attendance going back to fifth or sixth grade. The classic example was one girl that had missed many, many days of school, sometimes as many as 100 in one school year. By the time she got to our school, she had begun to realize that she needed to take school more seriously, worked hard with us, returned to the traditional high school for the last semester of her senior year and graduated. Her best friend was Veronica, the girl who died in that car crash that I spoke of earlier. It appeared that Veronica's death had motivated her to improve her life. She was a very bright young woman and once settled found that the academic portion of going to school just wasn't that challenging. It is my wish that her story had a happy ending, but no. Near the end of my years as a teacher, she showed up at my school one afternoon with her son. She introduced him and said, "Mr. O, I need your help". I asked her what I could do. She just looked at the floor and said, "I can't get him to go to school." The county eventually ran out of patience with her and she spent a few days in jail. By the time of my retirement, her son still had not begun to attend school regularly.

There were three young men who were just ever so different from the rest of the students that we ever had. I will identify two of them by the phrases that they uttered constantly, "Puro Pedo" and "There it is there". Jose was an average looking young man, he just seemed to operate at a much slower speed than everybody else. He was never a troublemaker, he came to school nearly every day, sat at his desk and appeared to focus on whatever assigned tasks that we provided for him. Our school consisted of two classrooms and Jose would occasionally get up from his desk, walk up to the pencil sharpener, bring his pencil to a very sharp edge, walk quietly into the next classroom. Pass by several students without saying a word to anyone, continue on his way back into his original classroom, sit down at his desk and continue his methodical approach to completing his work for the day. This went on day after day, week after week, all school year long. Unfortunately, he wasn't turning in very many completed assignments and did not make much progress toward graduation. He just did not raise any red flags during the school day, never coming to the attention of any staff member. In those days, the staff would send to each student's home, a monthly report on how the young person was doing. The report included their attendance at school, the number of times that they had clocked-in late and the amount of credits that they had earned toward graduation that month. We also wrote a note to each parent in either English or Spanish, about our observations of the student. We gave special attention to making these notes as positive as possible. We often had to be as creative as we could be to mention how the student was making progress in some area. When it came to writing notes about Jose, there just wasn't much that we could say except that he was in class, on time and didn't cause any difficulties for anyone at school. Whenever we talked to Jose concerning how he was doing and his lack of academic progress, all he would say was "Puro Pedo". This, of course in Spanish means "it is all for nothing". It appeared that he had adopted this as his philosophy of life. I truly wish that I had been able to keep in touch with him. On many occasions over the years, I have been surprised to find out that many of these young people came out of the "fog on adolescence" and made a life for themselves. They found jobs and careers, settled down with a partner, raised children and paid their taxes. I would love to hear that about Jose.

The second lovable character was named Albert. At first glance, it was very difficult to tell whether Albert was either stoned most of the time or simply the most mellow person you ever met. I believe that his mellowness was the reason he came to our school to begin with. He never broke out of this laid-back style and while this can be a positive characteristic in life, it also made it difficult for him to focus on completing schoolwork. This put him behind in his classes at the traditional high school and when he arrived on our campus, he maintained his lack of productivity in completing assignments. What made him so lovable was that whenever anyone would make a comment in the classroom, Albert would say softly, "There it is there." If one of the teachers criticized another student for their unacceptable behavior, Albert would say, "There it is there." If another student would blurt out a comment, Albert would say, "There it is there." No one, not staff or students ever resented Albert's phrase. He was so well liked that everyone just sort of expected him to contribute his now famous comment. Albert stayed at our school a couple of years. He never graduated but he seemed to be satisfied to be a part of the group and even had some recognition for his comments by the other students. I eventually became award of something else that Albert was known for in the community. He loved to work on repairing and improving old cars. He was well known at the local car shows for his amazing vehicles. The relatively little-known world of "Low Rider" car people includes a good number of people young and old. Albert had attained quite some status there.

Finally, the last lovable character that I include in this category was a little guy named Larry. Larry had one of those up-tempo personalities. He was always fun to be around and all of the students liked him. He was also widely disliked by many teachers at the traditional high school because of his hyper behavior, he could be extremely disruptive in a typical, crowded classroom. The other thing that made him so lovable was that on the previous Fourth of July, he had tried to throw an M80 firework and it went off in his hand, blowing three of his fingers off. The movie Stand and Deliver was very popular that year and in it there was a character who used his fingers to assist him in counting. The teacher, Jaime Escalante (played by Edward James Olmos) nicknamed the student "Fingerman". When Larry enrolled in our school, I immediately placed the nickname "Fingerman" on him. He didn't seem to mind, it added to his status as the class clown.

SHELLY

One of the reasons that I got into teaching in the first place was that I wanted to coach sports. Being an athlete had been a hugely important part of my childhood and adolescence and I hoped to continue those feeling by providing a positive experience for other young athletes. As early as 1967, I coached junior high school basketball teams in Oxnard and West Los Angeles. I was able to continue this by coaching football and basketball at the high school level in Ventura County. Eventually, I found myself coaching Girls Basketball and over a twelve-year period we had quite a bit of success. My time in coaching the young ladies coincided with the passage of Title Nine in California. This law leveled the playing field between girls' and boys, sports requiring equal funding for each. This had the effect of raising interest in the attention given to the girl's efforts. After I retired from coaching in 1994, I continued to stay in touch with many of the former players, mostly through Facebook. I am proud to say that I have been able to sustain friendly relationships with many of them. Recently, I came across a name that I had not heard for more than thirty years. Her name is Michelle Swift. When she played on teams that I coached in the early 1980's she went by Shelly. Shelly was a talented, hard-working athlete, her biggest attribute was her intensity while playing on the court. That made her an outstanding defensive player. Whenever I put her into a game, I knew that the girl that she was guarding was going to struggle and not be as effective as normal. Shelly always worked hard whether in a practice or game. Unfortunately, her time on the team came to an abrupt end during her junior year. One morning, during Winter Vacation, Shelly didn't come to practice. All of the players knew that this was unacceptable. I called her at home later that day and asked why she was missing. She hesitated for a moment and said, "It's vacation and I decided to go Christmas shopping with my friends." I quickly told her that I hope that she had a good time and to turn her uniform in on Monday. I didn't see her much after that but when I did, there was never any animosity. As I say, I had not seen nor heard anything about Shelly for many years until I saw her name that day on Facebook. I sent her a message and she responded almost immediately. She was very friendly and asked about what I had been doing lately. I filled her in and asked what she was doing. She explained that she now worked for NASA in Houston. I wrote back that I didn't know she had an interest in science. She then said, "I'm a cyber intelligence analyst. "Ha ha, no science in that" she wrote back. "I learned those skills when I joined the Army." I was surprised and yet, not so much. I guess that intensity on the basketball court found a new avenue for her. She was another former student/athlete to be proud of.

TONY

He was just an extremely good looking, friendly young man who was also a good athlete. He could have had a successful career playing a variety of sports at the high school, but Tony could never stay eligible academically. After a couple of years of struggle at the local high school, he was sent to our alternative school to try to catch-up on his classes. He always seemed to be bright enough to complete the required school-work but he seldom found the ability to focus and succeed. I never witnessed him cause trouble and he always treated the staff at our school with respect. He was joined at our school by his sister and she seemed to be very much like her brother in abilities but also lacked much enthusiasm for learning. When Tony turned eighteen, he was asked to leave our school to make room for a new student who needed our help. I did not see Tony very often for the next couple of years and when his younger brother came to us, I made contact once again with the family. Tony's brother seemed to be so much like him that I could see so many negative patterns emerge. After all these years, I had a good relationship with Tony's mother and once again saw her frustration. One morning Tony's mother called me. I thought she was going to tell me about her frustrations with the third child to come to our school. I was instead surprised to hear her crying uncontrollably. I asked her what had happened and she said, "Tony's dead, the drugs finally got him." Here, once again was a promising life lost to drugs. Frustration on the part of teachers can sometimes be overwhelming.

MARIANNE

In 1977 I began a new teaching position at a small Catholic Elementary School in West Los Angeles. When I was hired, the Principal asked me if I would take on the roles of Athletic Director and Coach in addition to my being the eighth-grade teacher. She wanted to expand the availability of sports programs offered to the students. This was my first full time teaching position. During the school day, I taught English, Science and Social Studies each morning. After lunch, I taught P.E. to Kindergarten through Eighth Grade. It was a tremendous stretch between that wide range in ages and abilities. By adding the after-school responsibilities, Sister was getting quite a bargain, considering that I was paid $610 a month. During the year and a half that I worked there, the school fielded and eighth grade as well as a seventh grade flag football team, a boy's basketball team and a girl's softball team. In the Spring, the Southern California Catholic Youth Organization announced that a region wide Track and Field Meet would be held in East Los Angeles. I announced to the student body that I was taking sign-ups. We had several good athletes at the school so I recruited around twenty students to participate. We had a few good sprinters and an excellent distance runner on the boy's team. There were five good sprinters on the girl's team and we formed a very competitive 400 meter relay team. I held practices for three weeks in a local park. On the day of the meet, there were several thousand people in attendance with probably 500 athletes competing. The day was going well and our athletes were enjoying themselves and were quite successful. When the 400 meter girl's race was called, three of the girls were very excited and were completing their warm-ups when I noticed one of them was just standing off to the side, not warming-up. Her name was Marianne. I walked up to her and asked if she was alright. She just stared at me, finally saying, "There's too many people here." She had completely panicked, unable to move. Marianne's typical attitude was that she was very cool, unflappable. Several times over the year, I had to reprimand her for being difficult to get along with both in the classroom and as an athlete. At that moment, there at the track meet, her façade had completely crumbled. I took her aside and told her to not worry about it, she wouldn't have to run that day. Luckily, we had another girl, her sister Elena, who was able to step-up and run in the race. The team did very well and I told them that I was proud of them. Marianne and I never discussed the event again.

The other time that I coached a track and field team was at a junior high school in Oxnard. A long time P.E. teacher at the school asked if I would be interested in helping with the girl's team. The school had a number of very talented athletes, especially sprinters and long-distance runners. I made the announcement that I would be holding tryouts for high jumpers in the activity room after school. The veteran coach came by to give me a hand in choosing a few high jumpers. He showed them how to do some of the traditional techniques such as The "Western Roll" and "The scissors kick" and gave them a few pointers. Eventually, a young student named Jody stepped-up to make her attempt. Instead of using the old style of jumping, she ran up and performed a perfect "Fosbury Flop". This style had only been around for a few years, developed by a college high jumper named Dick Fosbury and was highly controversial. Instead of rolling over the bar face first, the "flop" that Jody used meant that she would run up to the bar, turn her back to the bar jump up, kicking her legs over her head and land on her back. The old coach was very surprised to see Jody do this and said, "Oh, you know how to do the flop. Very good." She competed for the school the entire season and did very well, winning several meets and impressing a lot of people. It turned out that the season was the end of her competitive career. She never competed in high school. She was an excellent student and although I never saw her again, I am certain that she was very success in her life. The way she jumped that first day at the tryout, listening respectfully to the old coach, and then performing the way she wanted to with so much confidence was so impressive to me.

I was also looking for other potential athletes who could compete in other events. One day in class, I noticed a young lady, actually a close friend of Jody's, who seemed to have the right body type to be a shot putter. Her name was Lynn and she was a very nice, mild tempered, hard-working student. I called her aside one afternoon and asked if she had ever tried to throw the shot. She said she had not and when I asked her if she would like to give it a try, she said she would. Shot putting was the only track and field event that I had ever participated in when I was in junior high. It came very easily to me. I worked with her for a few minutes one day at practice and she learned very quickly. She competed the entire season for the team and won several meets. She seemed to really enjoy competing and she and Jody worked very hard and really did well. I was very proud of both of them. Lynn also never crossed my path again. I moved on to another school district the next year. Again, like Jody, I feel certain that she has had a successful life.

PAUL

There were a few occasions over the years at the alternative school that enough money was found in the school budget to take the students enrolled in our school on a field trip. We were able to take them to the beach, the L.A. County museums including the IMAX theater and the Southern California Edison Power Plant in Oxnard. The fact that these students had lived most of their lives in a small, rural community made any chance to see the "bigger world" quite rewarding. By far the favorite trip for our students was to Universal Studios. To justify these trips, we had to come up with a bona fide teaching goal. We used exposure to career opportunities, economic outcomes and even an example of earthquake preparedness to justify the trips. The students always enjoyed the trips, even if they did not always understand our educational goals. For the most part, they were well behaved, mostly because the staff spent a great deal of time and effort preparing them for the potential outcomes of "dumb choices". Mr. Muchisky always read them the riot act, telling the students that "You are not in your small town now, this is Los Angeles. You will get caught and you will spend some time in the L.A. Juvenile Hall". This was usually enough to keep them in line and out of trouble. Of course, there was this one time when one of our students just had to test the warnings. His name was Paul and, you see there was this shopping area just outside of Universal Studios called City Walk. It contained numerous restaurants and shops where various souvenirs and other items were on display. Paul and a group of fellow students were walking around, looking at the items on display when he spotted a table of phone pagers sitting on a table. There were no employees from the store in sight, so Paul decided to take one, just one. In Paul's hometown there were no surveillance cameras in the stores so he was very, very surprised when he had walked only a few feet from the store and an employee suddenly put a vice like grip on his shoulder and said, "empty out your pockets, young man". Now we had told the students to return to the bus at exactly 1:30 pm. When the staff arrived at the bus a few minutes before the designated time, we knew nothing of Paul's detainment. A few students joined us at the bus, laughing as they got close. When we asked about the laughing, the students said, "Paul got arrested for shop-lifting". While the rest of the staff waited at the bus for the returning students Mr. Muchisky went off in search of Paul. He returned a few minutes later saying that he had found Paul in the holding cell inside Universal Studios, crying. He said that Paul just couldn't believe that he had gotten caught. He also informed us that the park security officers had called Paul's mother and told her to either come and retrieve him or he would be taken to Juvenile Hall in downtown Los Angeles. She did and a few days later Paul returned to school, to the teasing delight of the students. They were merciless. It was also at that time that we heard that a few of our students had dared Paul that day to try to steal the pager.

    We took the students a few years later to another trip to Universal Studios. On that day, the other two staff members whom I had joined to chaperone the students had to leave early to go coach a baseball game. Before the students left the bus they were given the same instructions about behavior and the time to return to the bus. I returned to the bus a little before 1:30 and as the other staff members had already left for the game, it fell to me to check all of the students back in before leaving. By 1:30 all but about four students had boarded the bus. By 1:40 the four missing students still had not returned. As I looked back over the faces of the students sitting quietly, I could almost hear them saying, "Well, we're here, you said 1:30, what are you going to do now?" I decided to leave the four students there at Universal Studios and just head for home. When we returned home, I called the parents of the four students and told them that they would have to go pick-up their children in Los Angeles. The parents were not happy and the Principal was also not happy the next day when he got to school. He had received several phone calls the night before and I was in the doghouse for quite a while. Needless to say, that was the end of the field trips at that school.

Writing about these field trips reminds me of others that I participated in during my career. The first was at a small Parochial school in West Los Angeles. The Principal, Sister Aurora, always seemed to be able to come up with funding for trips. Nearly all of the students enrolled at the school were from very low-income families. Sister saw the value of these opportunities for the students to get out and see other areas of the city that would not have be available to the students and their families. One day she came to me and said that she had received tickets for the entire eighth grade class, all 32 of them, to go to The Los Angeles County Museum to see the traveling exhibit of the King Tut collection. She was also going to provide a bus to take us and even invited four adults to help me supervise the kids. On a nice Spring day, we boarded the bus. It was rather warm, typical for the L.A. area that time of year. The bus driver told me that he was going to stick to the surface streets since we only had to travel about six miles. That meant that the trip would be simple but, he (and I) didn't realize how warm it was and that we would be driving in slow, stop and go traffic. That probably would not have been a problem except that he ordered the students to keep the windows up. By the time we arrived at the museum, several of the students became nauseated. As the students stood up in the aisle to leave the bus, I looked back and noticed one young man with a panicked look on his face and his cheeks completely inflated, obviously holding back a mouth full of vomit. He approached me and I reflexively pushed him away and into the center of the aisle. At that moment his mouth burst open and he puked all over the back of a female student in front of him. I will never forget the shocked look on her face, not knowing at that moment what had actually happened to her. Fortunately, two of the women chaperones stepped up to help and clean her up. The King Tut exhibition was fascinating and the students really enjoyed it, except for the vomit victim. The pukee completely recovered and very little more was eve said about the accident.

As I have mentioned before, I coached several sports during my career as a teacher. One year, at the end of the basketball season, the student-athletes at the junior high school where I was working were invited to a free trip to an amusement park in Santa Clarita. All of the teams went along with the cheerleaders. In addition, the MEChA club (a group that was organized to promote unity and empowerment among young Hispanic students) from the school was included. In all three buses were taken for the trip and we all arrived at the park at the same time. Now, all of these students, athletes, cheerleaders and club members were enrolled at the same school. Many of them were even related. I expected all of them to be treated the same as we entered the amusement park. I was shocked to see the park security take the MEChA club members aside and search every one of them while allowing the students that I was supervising to enter the park undisturbed. I suppose I should have known better.

On another occasion, one year the staff from our alternative school took the students from our school to the IMAX theater in Exposition Park, Los Angeles. We were going to see a documentary about space travel, thereby meeting our educational criteria. While waiting for the movie to begin, the students and staff waited in the outdoor courtyard of the theater. The area was filled with homeless people and our students enjoyed watching and interacting with them even more that the movie. Being raised in such a small, rural community, the students were intrigued by the street people. It was an unintended lesson.

PHIL CATALANO AND BILL PUTMAN

During my thirty-year teaching career, I worked with fourteen different supervisors/principals. Some were supportive, easy to work with, some were nearly impossible to deal with and some were mostly not there, both emotionally and physically. They seemed to be more interested in attending meetings and off campus events. Two men stand out in my mind as exceptional, true professionals. They were Phil Catalano and Bill Putman. Both were real veteran educators. Bill had worked for many years as a high school counselor. He really knew the students and understood their struggles. Before I arrived, he had also worked as a principal at a comprehensive high school and at an elementary school. When he came to our alternative school, he was nearing the end of his lengthy career. He was looking forward to retirement but he was also determined to work hard to improve the school. Phil had stated as a music teacher at a comprehensive high school and later moved into administration as a vice-principal at a middle school. The attribute that I appreciated the most in both of these men was that they were very supportive of the teachers needs and requests. Students at an alternative school can be very challenging and require a great deal of creative interventions. Many times Bill and Phil would meet with the staff and assist us in the development of new programs to meet the needs of both students and staff. Both men always sought our input in response to making changes at the school. Some students had special academic needs that had led to their being transferred to our school. Most of the time, these two men met with us, sought our input in making academic changes in order to improve the student's learning needs and then provided whatever training and new materials that were required. I always felt good about this team approach. A few other administrators had demonstrated that it was their job to push some new program down the student's (and teachers) throats because he or she believed they knew the best way to do things. The other significant characteristic about these two great educators was their commitment to becoming involved in the lives of the students. One morning, Bill received a phone call from one of our students that she was having a problem with her mother. All Bill said was, "I'll be right there". When he returned to school about an hour later, Bill told us that the student and her mother were at a local motel where the mother was drunk and causing a disturbance. He said that when he knocked on the motel room door, the student answered and let him into the room. The student's mother was lying on the bed naked and thrashing about yelling and cursing. Bill said that he didn't know what to do so he and the student wrapped the mother up in a blanket and he sat and talked to both of them, calming the situation. As he told us this story, he appeared to blush and was quite embarrassed.

When Phil was our principal, one afternoon, as our students were leaving campus, the staff was outside supervising the students. At one point, students from the nearby junior high school were passing by in the opposite direction in front of our classrooms. Phil and I were standing together and we observed one of the younger students hand a small bag of marijuana to one of our students. I then saw Phil charge down the walkway, chasing the student with the bag. Everyone, students and staff stopped and watched as Phil chased the student down the hill and into the lemon orchard pursuing the student. We watched as both the student and Phil disappeared into the trees. Eventually, Phil returned to the school with the bag in his hand. He said that the student had dropped the bag and fled the area. Phil called the police and accompanied the officer to go find the student and he was arrested and sent to juvenile hall. The other students were laughing as Phil ran through the orchards but later, they said how impressed they were at "Mister Cat's" commitment.

A couple of years later, Phil and I attended a conference in Santa Maria where staff from several alternative schools gathered to share some of the innovative programs that were successful for them. In addition to discussing the textbooks and computer software that they used, one school presented information about their camping excursion class. They told us about taking small groups of their students out into the wilderness and how they felt the lessons learned by the students were so important. As we drove home that afternoon, Phil and I discussed how we felt the camping class could be useful to our students. Over the next few weeks we worked on how we might adapt the class to be something we could submit for approval to our school board. From the beginning, we sought Owen's input into the planning. We knew that we would be able to take only a maximum of about eight students. Phil and I would drive, taking students in his van and one of the school district vans. That would mean that Owen would be responsible for the students remaining at the school with the help of a substitute teacher. Together, we selected eight students that we felt would benefit from such an experience as well as be cooperative and participate in the team atmosphere. Phil brought his van and towed his pop-up trailer. I drove one of the school vans. As the students boarded the vans, Phil and I searched the student's luggage. Three of the students were female, so we had our school secretary search them as Phil and I patted down the boys. The trip was planned for three days and two nights, so as we left town, we stopped at the local grocery to pick-up enough food to feed eight teenage eating machines as well as two over-weight teachers. When we arrived at Sycamore Canyon State Park, just north of Malibu, we supervised as the students set-up the two tents where the boys would sleep. I had a couple of students help me remove two rows of seats in the school van which gave the three girls enough room to roll out their sleeping bags. Phil and I set up his pop-up trailer where we would sleep. When everything was ready, including the purchase of some firewood for a nightly campfire, we called everyone together for a meeting. We laid out some basic ground rules and expressed to the students what we expected of them over the next few days. We didn't tell the students at the time but Phil and I had previously decided that our goal for this trip was to observe the students as to how they inter-acted with each other particularly in how they pitched-in to help prepare meals and clean-up each day. Phil and I sat back and allowed the students to plan the meals, designate who would do the cooking and who would clean-up after each meal. From the beginning, we noticed that certain individuals just naturally took charge while most of the others did not hesitate to help out. One of the girls, whom everyone called La Shorty took over from the beginning. A couple of the others, Mike and Gino patiently demonstrated how to set-up the tents and prepare the food for cooking to those who had little experience in camping. On the first day in the campground, by the time everything was set up and the fantastic evening meal was finished, there was just enough time to have everybody enjoy a nice campfire in the big pit. Everyone was tired after the trip, the making of dinner and the clean-up afterward. The students got to their chosen sleeping spots and for the most part fell asleep early. The next day, after a good breakfast, again planned and cooked by the students, they chose to take a walk and become familiar with the campground. After lunch, Mike really began to show his camping experience. He led the students on a two-hour hike into the local foothills. Later, as a group of students under the leadership of La Shorty made dinner, Mike again demonstrated his skills. He took out a sling shot, fired a pebble at a squirrel about forty yards away, killed it, skinned it and cooked the meat over an open fire. I told him, "Mike if there is ever a disaster, I'm following you to safety". The next day we had a visit from our school counselor, Walter. He led the students in a discussion about how their lives were going. The counselor did this regularly at our school but it was an even more effective meeting out in the woods. One of the topics that I remember the students discussing was how they had begun to view other students in the group differently while camping than they had before. This really surprised me because these young people lived in a very small town and had known each other most of their lives. They had attended the same schools for years and still they did not truIy understand nor accept many of their classmates. It took an experience out of town, in a very relaxing setting to allow such acceptance. Of course, the other gratifying aspect was how well they got along and shared responsibility during the trip. Phil and I were pleased with the entire experiment. We expressed this to them and rewarded each student some elective credits toward graduation. The entire experience had been a tremendous success and for several years thereafter, students asked me when the next camping trip would take place. Unfortunately, Phil left our school the next year to become the Principal at the local junior high school. A couple of years later, Phil died from a heart attack. He left a tremendous impact on the students he worked with and the community in general. None of the Principals who followed him at our school ever expressed an interest in following-up on the camping trip.

RUDY

Rudy was a rather average looking young man who came to our school when he was sixteen years old. He had been falling behind ever since he first attended high school, never making any more than the least effort in his schoolwork. When he started with us, he was never a disruptive person. He just sat back in the classroom and observed the other students. He did seem to have a problem getting to school on time and missed more days of school than he should. Those were common characteristics of the students attending our school. The thing that made him memorable to me is that he became a father at a very early age and more often than what was typical. Two of our female students were apparently extremely attracted to Rudy. They were good friends having grown up together in the same small town. Over the next few years, even after Rudy no longer attended our school, he again and again got the two friends pregnant. One of the girls told me one afternoon that Rudy had told each of the girls, "I'm going to keep getting you two pregnant until one of you gives me a son". I later heard that he was making similar efforts with other young ladies in our community. Unfortunately for the two girls, their children, the community and the Welfare System in general, a total of seven children were born before he achieved his stated goal. Thanks Rudy. As for the girls, the last time I saw one of them, I was told that they have remained close friends. A couple of years later, Rudy was involved in a gang fight. Several young men joined in the battle and Rudy was stabbed to death in the street in front of his girlfriends and even a couple of his children.

C- SCHOOL SOFTBALL

In the Spring of 1985 Owen and I met with several other teachers from alternative education high schools in Ventura County. For the previous few years, there had been discussions about the possibility of establishing a slow-pitch softball league in which our students could compete with students from other schools similar to ours. Fillmore, the town where our school was located has a long history of baseball (and softball) being very popular and successful. I have seen photographs of Fillmore baseball teams from as early as 1910. A couple of major league players graduated for the local comprehensive high school. At this meeting it was decided to establish some special rules. First, we decided to have a minimum of two girls on each team. Fillmore always had several excellent girl softball players and some of them attended our school. The other rule that we decided upon was that the teams would have one of their own players pitch to their team. That eliminated any controversy over calling balls and strikes. The first year of league play had a total of six schools that participated, Oxnard, Ventura, Conejo Valley, Oak Park, Moorpark and Fillmore. The first three schools had enrollments of more than two hundred students. Oak Park, Moorpark and Fillmore had enrollments of less than forty students. That initial season, we played games against the five other schools. Our students had a very good time and even won a couple of games. It was a good opportunity for our students to get out of town, meet students from other alternatives high schools and once again demonstrate that they had learned how to take on and complete a commitment. After a couple of seasons, the representatives of the six member schools got together again and made the decision to hold an end of season tournament. It was decided to hold a on-day tournament and award a perpetual trophy that would be held by the winner for one year. The tournament would be played as a one pitch tournament. That meant that each batter would receive one pitch. If they failed to swing or swung and missed the ball or even fouled the ball off, they were called out. Since each team provided their own pitcher, the batter expected the pitch to be at least hit-able. The games went very quickly, the seven innings usually being completed in thirty minutes or less. The games began at 9:00 in the morning and the tournament was normally completed by noon. It was always an amazing sight to observe 60 or 70 young people with the worst reputations for being able to ger along, enjoy themselves playing softball on a Spring day. The hosting school then put on a barbecue for all of the players and the championship trophy was awarded. It was always a memorable event and our students always enjoyed it. Fillmore even won the tournament one year. Owen and I agreed that the use of athletic competition had a significant effect on our students. It is tremendously difficult to focus and put great effort into playing a sport when your self-esteem has been damaged by a lack of success in school or life in general. This was the case with many of our students, they were in the position that they were due to mistakes that they had made and some were there because some teachers, office workers and administrators had been abusive to them in the past. The entire staff at our school was always very proud of our students when they found a way to succeed, to overcome obstacles, despite past difficulties.

THE BLACK WIDOW

The *Latrodectus mactans* or Black Widow Spider, is known for a behavior called "sexual cannibalism" in which after mating, the female will kill and consume her partner. In the Spring of 1984, a new female student enrolled at our school. She was the youngest student ever to come to our school, only fourteen years of age, still a ninth grader. From the first few weeks, Owen and I noticed that she was far above average in intelligence, capable of completing most of the academic tasks that we placed before her. The reason that she was sent to our school was her disruptive behavior in the classroom. She was an only child without much discipline at home and often refused to follow the direction of any adult. We also noticed that her interactions with our male students was extremely aggressive. She was an attractive young lady and time and again, the boys would become pursue her, make advances and after a day or two, emerge substantially damaged emotionally. They seemed to be in a dazed, comalike state. In a manner similar to the Black Widow Spider, the boys were devoured and returned to the masses frail and emaciated. We observed this behavior several times over the next few school years. When we investigated her personal history, we found that her world was dominated by women. Her father was not in the picture and she lived with her mother and grandmother. She acted in an aggressive, flirtatious manner with nearly every male she encountered. When it came to her dealings with the adult staff members, she would become angry and verbally abusive with little provocation. I remember her use of what to her was the ultimate insult when disagreeing with the male staff members, "Leave me alone, OLD MAN!" She was quite a challenge for the entire staff, male and female. She had become so used to getting her own way at home that she became almost impossible to work with at school. It was interesting to observe how the older girls at our school dealt with her. For the most part, they ignored her directly, complaining to the staff about her disruptive actions. As new girls came to our school, they too were attracted to her strong-willed personality. Together they formed a small clique. Many of the new boys also fell for her seductive ways. The now experienced victims were interesting to watch as they just sat in their desks and slowly shook their heads, with a far-away look in their eyes chuckling to themselves.

After a couple of years at our school, The Black Widow began to show some improvement in her behavior. I like to think that the structure and support that we provided began to help her begin to make progress. She began to complete more schoolwork, she barked at staff members less and less and just seemed to become a nicer person. It's amazing how a little maturity, a reduced flow of hormones, mixed with a more stable school experience will change some young people. She was eventually able to earn a high school diploma and settled in Oklahoma. She has a daughter of her own now and I wonder if that relationship is more successful. I communicated with her a few years ago. After catching-up with me on her life, she said, "You know, Mr. O, I'm glad that you came into my life exactly when I needed someone to help me. Thank you." Success in education is not always about academics.

BAM BAM

Even before I was hired as a teacher, I coached basketball. Beginning in 1967, I coached junior high school and high school boy's teams. In 1982, I was hired at the alternative school in Fillmore, CA. I inquired about a basketball coaching position at the local comprehensive high school. When I was told that the only position available was for the girl's junior varsity team, I thought, coaching is coaching I'll give it a try. The varsity coach was a very experienced man named Don Hoover. He was a very nice person but he too had very little experience coaching girls. That first season was a real challenge. There were several good female athletes that tried out for the team but the main sport of interest at that time was softball. The team won only four of the eleven games we played. On the positive side, the girls were very enthusiastic and really wanted to learn about basketball. They were willing to work very hard at developing the necessary skills of the game and more importantly, they worked together very well and very supportive of my emphasis on "team basketball". During the summer after my first season, I organized a series of workouts and most of the girls were eager to participate. Their skill level greatly improved and as a result, the second season was a huge success. The team won sixteen of seventeen games and easily captured the league Junior varsity championship. The next season, Coach Hoover asked me to take over as the varsity coach. He offered to coach the JV team because, he said there were a few girls ready to play varsity level ball that he had had personal difficulty with while they were in the junior high school where he taught. I felt that I was ready to take on this new challenge and I already knew these girls and what they could become. Over the previous two years, several new girls had come into the program and I was very confident about our potential. It turned out that I was perhaps too confident. The higher skill level of play for varsity basketball was something that I wasn't prepared for as well. During my first year as a varsity coach, the team struggled and we won only six games. A few parents even asked me if I would be going back down to coach the junior varsity team again. I said no, that I believed this group of young ladies could become winners.

During the next summer, I again had the girls in the gym, continuing to work on improving. One afternoon, I was visiting my co-teacher Owen Muchisky and his daughter Deana. With her that day was her closest friend, April Ponce. At first glance, April appeared to be an average looking teenage girl. She was smaller and rather frail looking but I noticed something in her eyes and facial expression that was striking. She had a look of intensity that most people, young or old rarely possess. It was completely obvious to me that this young girl was a natural athlete. I asked her if she had ever played any sports. She said she had, mostly softball and some basketball. She seemed like a natural. Deana told me that April's nickname was "Bam Bam" because she and Deana were always together and at that time Deana's hair and ponytail looked very much like the Flintstones character "Pebbles". In the tv show, "Pebbles" and another character named "Bam Bam" were always together. All of Deana and April's school friends just thought it natural to give them those nicknames. I then told both girls that I was holding a basketball practice the next day at 2:00 pm and asked them if they would like to join in. I will never forget that scene. Practice the next day was just beginning when the gym door opened just a slight crack and in walked this diminutive, dark haired, thin girl. The other players were mostly Seniors and had been with me since they first entered high school. A couple of them looked at me with extremely quizzical expressions on their faces but said nothing. I directed the team to begin doing some lay-ups to begin the warm-up process. I motioned for April to join in and she didn't hesitate. I had learned early on that lay-ups were difficult for many girls. It took a great deal of coordination to dribble the ball toward the basket, step upward and skillfully let the ball out their hand and bank it off the backboard and into the basket. It took a lot of practice and some of the players never did accomplish it successfully. On her first try, April completed the task perfectly and the ball slipped through the net with a slight swoosh. I smiled as several of my veteran players jerked their heads and looked at me with their mouths open in surprise. A few minutes later, I had the girls do another drill where one player dribbled the ball down the court, did a jump stop and passed the ball to another girl running in the same direction. The second girl caught the ball, jumped in the air and put up about a ten-foot shot toward the basket. When April got the ball she dribbled, came to a perfect stop and made a quick, crisp pass to the other girl running down the court. It was performed like right out of a basketball textbook. Again, several girls turned to see my reaction. A few minutes later, it was April's turn to shoot the ball. She caught the ball with both hands, made a perfect jump stop, put up a shot while in perfect balance and swoosh! The ball went through the hoop, touching nothing else. One of my senior players, a girl who had been the team leader for three years, ran up to me and said, "she's good". I didn't say anything but I wanted to say, "Duh". After practice, several of the team members went up to April and congratulated her on her talent. One thing that I always enjoyed about coaching girls was that ego was rarely an issue. When they saw someone to knew how to play the game, they admired her and usually let her know it. Coaches always look forward to having the opportunity to coach someone who really gets what the coach is trying to teach. I think of it like the times a classroom teacher, in math or science finds a student in their class who is in complete synch with the teacher. The next summer, I found a basketball league in Oxnard that provided a chance for teams to play in actual games. I had been looking for such a league because I knew it would provide an excellent opportunity for my players to improve. I had about ten players who had expressed a wish to play in such games and once a week for six weeks I loaded them into my van and off we went. In addition to the team members, I also invited Deana and April. They were only going to be eighth graders in the fall but there were no rules keeping them out of off-season games. I was very pleased with the efforts of my team, they were going up against teams and players that were much more advanced than mine. The girls held their own and learned a lot about the game. During each game, I put Deana and April into the game, never mentioning to the other coaches that both girls were under-age. Both girls did very well and when the other coaches eventually found out about how young they were, they were shocked. Both girls worked very hard and developed quickly. Deana became a defensive specialist. Her competitive intensity made her eager to try and shut down her opponents. After each game, she would show me the numerous cuts and bruises that she wore as a badge of courage. She was able to maintain these abilities throughout her high school career. It was obvious that girls from other teams did not look forward to playing against her. She earned an Honorable Mention award for All Tri-Valley League at the end of her senior year. As for "Bam Bam", she was able to step right into varsity basketball her freshman year. I wanted to ease April into playing so I decided to not start her during pre-league games. Once league play started, I had her in there as much as possible. Over her four seasons as a leader of the program, April was everything that I had imagined that first day I met her. She was an outstanding ball handler, connected on more three-point shots than anyone around and even battled for every rebound, in spite of her lack of size.

As early as 1981 I had been a member of The National Association of Basketball Coaches. They offered several workshops each year as well as a convention at the Final Four tournament which was held in conjunction with the NCAA Basketball Tournament. I was able to attend three of the annual championship weekends, once in Seattle and twice in New Orleans. I always came away from these conferences with a few new, innovative ideas. After a conference in 1987, I wanted to try an idea that I had heard about. A college coach described something that he did every season with his team. He would hand a piece of paper to each of his players, telling them to rank in order each member of the team from most important to least. He felt that in this way, the players would develop an understanding of each player's role in making the team successful. After the second week of practice, I handed out papers to each of my fourteen players and instructed them as to what I wanted. The next day, I found thirteen papers on my desk with April's name appearing at the top. Every player was eager to express their belief that April was the most important member of the team. The only one who did not submit a paper was April "Bam Bam" Ponce. After practice I pulled April aside and asked her why she did not turn in a list. She looked me straight in the eyes and said, "I just couldn't be the judge of my teammates. I love them all the same". April became one of the greatest players in the history of the school. Her talent, hard work, defense, scoring and leadership abilities led to her being inducted into the school athletic hall of fame. For several years after she graduated, coaches and players from schools that she had played against would praise her play and ask me what she was doing. I wanted to do something special to honor this amazing young athlete. A friend from high school named Don Merrell had begun crafting beautiful blown glass trophies for a gymnastics program in Orange County. I asked him to make one with the figure of a female basketball player on it. At the end of season award ceremony, I presented it to April, calling it the BAM Award. Over the next several seasons, I chose a player who best exemplified the qualities that April Ponce had demonstrated during her brilliant four-year varsity basketball career. The memory of that first afternoon that "Bam Bam" walked into the gym remains with me to this day. April remains a close friend.

PANCHO VILLA

In 1985, Owen and I attended a conference in San Diego of The California Continuation Education Association. Educators from all over California, teachers, counselors, secretaries and administrators assembled to share and exchange programs and ideas that they were using in their alternative schools. We both enjoyed the opportunity to meet these people who worked with students that were very similar to those that we had in our school. Several hundred people attended this convention and we were able to bring some very interesting ideas back to our school. The other thing that we got from this conference was a list of contacts from the people we met. On the second night of the conference, after participating in workshops, viewing presentations and attending a nice dinner, we found ourselves sitting with a small group of teachers late in the evening in the hotel bar. As we were getting to know some of these new colleagues, some members began telling jokes. After a few minutes, one veteran teacher, a tall, Caucasian man wearing a black cowboy shirt, black slacks and a silver bolo tie launched into what turned out to be a quite memorable story. The man was in his mid-sixties and was obviously a veteran educator from the San Diego area. He turned to me and said, "Ask me if I know Pancho Villa." That brought several giggles from some of the teachers in the group. I decided to follow his lead and said, "Do you know Pancho Villa?" He followed by saying, "Do I know Pancho Villa?" More giggles followed and he then said, "One day I was hiking through the desert. The sun had just gone down and I had built a campfire to keep me warm through the night. A few minutes later a man on a horse rode up and when he got to me he said, what are you doing here? I said that I was tired and wanted to spend the night by the fire. Now, I recognized this man because he is very famous. Everybody knows Pancho Villa and that Pancho Villa is very dangerous man. Everyone also knows that he has a very strange sense of humor. I was frightened and didn't know what to do. As I sat there on the ground, I decided to just do whatever he told me to do. After a few minutes, Pancho Villa kicked the sides of his horse and the horse made caca on the ground. Pancho Villa pulled out his pistola and looked at me and said, "eat the caca". I didn't want to eat the caca but I was afraid so I ate the caca. As I stood there looking at Pancho Villa with caca dripping down my face, Pancho Villa started to laugh. He laughed and laughed and began to shake. He shook so much that he fell off his horse on the ground and the gun fell out of his hand. I picked-up the gun and said, Pancho Villa you eat the caca and he did. Do I know Pancho Villa? Hell, we had lunch together." The people in the bar that night roared with laughter. I don't remember the name of the teacher that told that story that night but I attended several more conventions of the CCEA over the remaining twenty-four years of my teaching career and remained friends with several of those teachers. In case you don't know already, alternative school teachers are a rare breed.

GRADUATION DAY

Over my thirty-year teaching career, I witnessed many graduation ceremonies. Graduation day is a very special, emotional event that everybody looks forward to for many years. For many immigrant parents, it is the fulfillment of a dream. The first one that I participated in as a teacher was at the first school where I taught . This was at a small Parochial elementary school in West Los Angeles. I had come in as the eighth-grade teacher at the beginning of the second semester. My predecessor had left unexpectedly during Christmas Break. The eighth-grade class had a total of sixteen members. I was very pleased to have an opportunity to be a full-time teacher but the first few weeks were difficult. I had almost no classroom experience, made a lot of mistakes and the students were not pleased to have to get used to a new instructor in their final year of pre-high school. The Principal, Sister Aurora was very supportive and helpful but then she was getting quite a bargain, paying me a total of $610 a month. As the end of the school year approached, the students and I were getting along very successfully and everyone was looking forward to the graduation. The vast majority of students in the school came from very poor, hard-working, often undocumented families. Many of the parents had little formal education in Mexico. The thing that

I will remember forever is the looks on the tear-stained faces of the parents. They were so happy to see that their children were going to be able to take advantage of the opportunities that had not been available to them in their homelands. That was one of the reasons that they had come to America.

When I began teaching in Oxnard at a junior high school, I was asked to help supervise the Promotion ceremony that was held at the end of the school year. The district and school administrators preferred to call this a promotion ceremony rather than a graduation in order to have the students and their families focus on a high school diploma. It was felt that graduating from high school was far more important for the student's future. Unfortunately, the families of many of the students did not see it that way. The students and their parents made a big fuss over finishing junior high school and spent a great deal of money on expensive dresses girls and suits for the boys. I remember watching many of the poor girls attempt to walk up the theater's narrow staircase in their huge, billowing dresses on their way to the stage to receive their certificate of promotion. I later heard that some families had even rented limousines for the students to ride in on their way to the ceremony. For many of these parents, it was an enormous expense that they could not readily afford.

By the time I started working at the alternative education program in Fillmore, the staff had decided to individualize each student's academic program. That meant that each student would be assigned the coursework that they would need to complete their studies. Textbooks were assigned, computer assignments were issued and the student was told that it was up to him or her to finish the work under the supervision of the staff of course. We further decided that when a student finished all of their assigned tasks, the school would hold a ceremony to award them their diploma. Family members were invited and a few school board members handed out the diploma. It was an ideal situation because the student and their family were made to feel even more special. I remember one student who barely made it to the ceremony on time because he was home cutting holes in his newly purchased white tee-shirt. Typical of the type of student at our school, that was just the way he wanted to look. Another young man stood in front of the entire school, friends, family and district board members and cried big, flowing tears, after staff members made some glowing comments on how proud we were of him he said sniffling, "I've never had so many people say so many nice things about me". This method also demonstrated to the other students in the school who were nearing the completion of their assigned coursework that it could be done. The school board members also enjoyed the relaxed, simplicity of the event. As a staff, we liked the system because we could honor the accomplishments of the students and have the opportunity to meet with the parents on such a positive note for a change. For many parents, visits to the school had traditionally been dreaded. They had tired of being called in to be told what their student had done wrong now. This was the way in which we held graduation for the first ten years that I was working at the school. Eventually, when other Principals came to the school, a single, more traditional type of ceremony was held. As students finished their assigned coursework during the school year, they had to wait until June to receive their diplomas. Typically, at that time, a dozen or so students would graduate as a group with perhaps a hundred to two hundred family members in attendance at an outdoor event or at the district theater. Owen and I never liked this more traditional approach. It just didn't seem as personal.

    In 2010 I decided that it was time for me to retire from teaching. Thirty years was enough and I was ready to travel and see the America. The Principal that final year asked me to make the keynote address at the graduation ceremony. I had done this several times in the past as Owen and I had alternated performing this task over the twenty-five years that we worked together. I was happy to do this because it was my final year working at the school. I wanted to take the opportunity to say thank you to not only the graduates but to the families as well. Over the years, many of the same families had sent their children to our school. By the time I retired, I was working with numerous second-generation students whose mom or dad had been my students many years before. I also gave me a chance to say good-bye to the City of Fillmore, thanking everyone for their support over the years. After I congratulated the graduating seniors, I finished with, "Tomorrow is my last day here in Fillmore. I just want to say this one more time, the students at Fillmore Community High School are the brightest, most hard working and personable young people that I have ever known. Goodbye." The next day, all of the remaining students at the school were assembled and each staff member (by that time we had four teachers on staff) made a few comments about how the year had gone and what they expected for the next year. The Principal asked me to speak last and I said, "I have really enjoyed being a part of this school and the successes you have had. You will always be in my heart."

THE HAUNTED HOUSE

I was always impressed by the students at Fillmore Community High School with their interest in contributing to the people of our town. They would often come to me and propose an activity directed at helping those people in Fillmore who needed assistance. During the very first year that I worked there, the students decided to do something for the residents living in the local Convalescent home. With the help of the staff, the students wrapped candy and gathered Happy Easter cards and took them to the elderly to give them a bright spot of a memory. On another occasion, they were able to talk the Principal, Phil Catalano, into wearing a Santa Claus suit and invited local parents to bring their children in to sit on Santa's lap for a photograph. Normally, families had to drive 25 miles to the shopping mall in Ventura to do this' In addition, before every Christmas vacation, the students chose one of the families in need and donated a Christmas tree along with some decorations. One Fall, a group of students headed by Sonia Gonzalez, came to me and said they would like to put on a Halloween Haunted House in the classroom one evening. About twenty students gathered and planned out a pathway through the school holding various surprise stations. They constructed cardboard tunnels, curtains that hid doorways and placed desks and chairs around the two classrooms that were used to funnel the children into open areas that contained our costumed students. When the "victims" came into the open areas, our students would shout and jump out trying to scare the kids. The lights in the classrooms were off and the students had placed bright, flashing lights that kept the children off guard. In order to get the kids moving, one of our students had put on a hockey mask and was chasing the little ones with an electric chain saw (without the chain). We had approximately fifty "victims" and they all had a great time. I was proud of my students because they planned the event, participated enthusiastically in it and cleaned-up afterward. For several years, I was told by students that came to the school that they remembered being there for the Haunted House when they were children.

THE PENNY CARNIVAL

While living in Fillmore, Sylvia and I became friends with a local woman named Candi Tovar. She worked at the local grocery store and supervised a youth group at one of the churches in town. In those days, the city of Fillmore had no recreation department which meant that local children and teenagers had absolutely nothing to do during the long, hot summer days. One evening, Candi came over to our house and we discussed planning a free activity for the community. I told Sylvia and Candi how, when I worked as a recreation leader in Sunnyvale, CA, the staff put on a Penny Carnival for local children. A Penny Carnival is a variety of fun, simple games where children paid a penny to play and if they didn't have any money, the staff would give them a handful. We organized a planning meeting where Candi brought a few of her youth group members and I invited a group of my students from "C" School. Together we developed a series of game stations that included a fishing booth, a knock down the bowling pins with a softball, a toilet seat was set-up on end and the player had to throw a roll of toilet paper through it, a game where the player used a golf putter to knock a golf ball into a hole and a few other silly contests, a lollipop tree where children could pay a penny and could pick a lollipop, and a few other fun games. Several local businesses and individuals donated auction items and money. The Fillmore Optimist Club donated money and the supermarket where Candi worked donated a box of oranges that we sliced and gave to the kids. On the day of the carnival, a dozen friends and local citizens came and assisted in running the event. Candi and I went to Anaheim a few days before the carnival and bought $300 worth toys that we gave away as prizes. Approximately two hundred and fifty local children attended and had a wonderful time. As with The Haunted House, for years afterward, young people came up to me and said how much they enjoyed The Penny Carnival.

LONI

Loni Larson was just a special athlete. She could run, jump and make every athletic move that any basketball coach could ever ask for. Her father, Bruce Larson was a teacher at the local middle school. He had an extensive background in sports as a player and a coach. My first school year in Fillmore I met him and he was a very friendly man who welcomed me to Fillmore. His older daughter Marcie played on the first team that I coached. She was also a hard-working athlete who found success in Track and Field as a shot putter. Bruce told me that he was very proud of Marcie and that I had better be ready for daughter number two when she got to the high school. By the summer of her Sophomore year, I was taking her and the rest of my team to play in games in Oxnard. Since I had come from that area, I knew several coaches and I wanted my team to play against some of the most talented athletes in the county in order to measure their skills against more advanced teams. The mostly African-American, Samoan and Hispanic players were initially curious about this girl from Fillmore who looked like she had just arrived here from Sweden. It wasn't long before Loni won them over with her genuinely warm, friendly and accepting attitude. By the end of the next summer season, it seemed like everyone who competed against her or even saw her play just loved her style. In the four seasons that Loni played on my teams, I never heard her criticize anyone, ever. If a girl from another team attempted to get rough with her, Loni always fought back without ever losing her temper. If an official made a questionable call, Loni just kept on playing, always doing whatever it took to help her team win. For several years after she graduated, coaches and players who had played against her, would come up to me after the game and inquire as to how she was doing. Loni just always left a positive impression on everyone she met. She was an outstanding athlete in two other sports. In volleyball, with her tremendous jumping ability, she dominated the game. Her most successful sport was Track and Field. She succeeded at every event she entered but was especially dominant at the two hurdle events. She was a C.I.F. champion four years consecutively in the 400 meter hurdles and three years in the 110 meter hurdles, placing second once. Many young people with all that athletic ability might have exhibited some attitude issues. Loni always had the same wide grin on her face, always eager to learn something new about athletics and even more interested in how the team was doing. After graduation, Loni attended Cal Poly San Luis Obispo and had a great deal of success as a Heptathlon competitor. After completing her degree there, she earned a Master's Degree in Marriage and Family Therapy. She married and has five children. She remains happily married to this day.

COACH JOHN WOODEN

When I was a Sophomore in high school, the famous basketball Coach John Wooden of U.C.L.A. was a guest speaker at our annual sports banquet. This was in 1964 and The Bruins were in the middle of their golden age of winning National Championships. I remember his speech that night as he spoke about his "Pyramid of Success". For a person of such diminutive stature, he was mighty impressive, relating how a balance of academic and athletic emphasis was so important far beyond the athletic fields and gymnasiums. Another aspect that impressed me was that he was so familiar with the accomplishments of my high school Santa Clara High School and Coach Lou Cvijanovich. With all that he had on going on in his life, he had been keeping his eye on The Saints. Many years later, I was coaching high school basketball in Oxnard. After our season ended, the coaching staff decided to join The National Association of Basketball Coaches Association and attend their annual convention at the Final Four. This was 1984 and the games and convention were to be held in Seattle, Washington. We had a great time meeting with coaches from all over the world as well as attending games and workshops. As usual, the games were played on Saturday, a double header, with the final game held on Monday night. That left us with little to do on Sunday but one of the coaches that I was traveling with had previously met Coach Wooden, who happened to also be attending the convention. We were invited to take a walk with Coach Sunday morning at 8:00 am. It was the chance of a lifetime and we all decided to take advantage of it. We met Coach and a couple of his friends in the lobby of our hotel and for the next forty-five minutes, we followed him through the streets of downtown Seattle, listening to his discussion of a multitude of topics none of which included anything about basketball. He talked about some of his thoughts on life, often engaging us for our opinions. When he asked me directly what my occupation was, he seemed very interested as I told him about teaching in a small, rural alternative high school. As the minutes flew by, I felt like I was absorbing the thoughts of some religious guru. He was warm and seemed to appreciate our presence. Much of the time, he looked down to concentrate on his steps while speaking just loud enough for his followers to listen. Just being in his presence felt like such an honor. Afterward, as I reviewed the experience with my fellow coaches, we all came to the same conclusion. Coach John Wooden could have been an outstanding success in whatever field he chose. Later, I did some research on his life. I found that he was born and raised in Hall, Indiana and had been a superior student/athlete in high school and college. When he found basketball, he committed himself to the game and was named to the All-America team three times while playing at Purdue University. In 1960 he was named to the Basketball Hall of Fame as a player and in 1973 he became the first person to be named to that honor both as a player and a coach. When I look back on the experience that day in Seattle, I laugh because I almost decided to sleep in and pass up that opportunity.

SHOW BUSINESS TEACHER

My first full-time teaching position was at a small Catholic Elementary School in West Los Angeles in 1977. As I have mentioned before, I was the eighth-grade teacher, teaching English, General Science, History and P.E. The school was located near Hollywood and several of the student's families were employed at internationally known Friars Club in Beverly Hills as waiters and serving staff. The students would often tell me stories that their parents had related to them about numerous well-known entertainers. These families often made a substantial financial income which placed them near middle class in status. Often, they had come to America poor and sometimes illegally. In addition, there were in my classes two students whose fathers worked in show business at that time. The first was named Barry. His father was a member of a well-known dance group from the 1940's that had performed all over the world. Barry would tell me stories about the many celebrities that he had met. Another student, named Walter, was the son of an actor who was one of my favorites from TV in a series called Homicide. Thinking back all these years later, I am still struck by the memory that all of these kids, children raised around fame and high income, were actually so easy going and regular in so many ways. I am certain that their parents worked extremely hard to keep them that way.

MARICRUZ

In my thirty years as a classroom teacher, there were some students that just made an impression on me because of their sweetness and friendliness. This was Maricruz. She never came into the classroom without a smile on her face and an attitude that quickly spread positivity throughout the school. In so many ways, she was just a typical young person. Learning was not the most important thing for her. Like so many of the young people that I dealt with, she made it through the week by looking forward to the weekends. Everybody liked her and I never saw her say or do anything that upset anyone, adolescent or adult, man or woman, boy or girl. She was not a superior student in the area of academics, making slow but steady progress toward earning her high school diploma. In the afternoons and early evening's she worked at a local pizza restaurant. I have no doubt that she contributed to her family's meager income. I had known her family for several years as her cousins, brothers and sisters enrolled in my classes. For the most part, they were similar to Maricruz, being friendly and popular but rarely motivated about school. I had heard that one of her brothers had gotten into trouble with the police because of drug and alcohol induced rages. He had always behaved himself when at school and he was an excellent athlete, playing on our school softball team. I witnessed some of this different personality one Spring at the downtown festival. He was talking to a couple of friends and appeared to have a great deal of trouble standing due to probable drug use. I was therefore not too surprised to see an article in the local newspaper on March 4, 2013 after I had retired and moved out of Fillmore. The headline read Fillmore man kills sister. The story went on to report that the young man had come home one evening extremely upset and when his mother tried to control him, he pushed her to the floor, injuring her. His sister, Maricruz stepped up to stop him and he beat and choked her, killing her. The family tragedy continued at a highly publicized trial where he was given a twenty-five year sentence. Another example of drugs destroying lives.

THE CLASSROOM COMPUTER MAN

Owen and I knew that it was going to be an interesting school year from day one. Our new Principal had never been a classroom teacher. In fact, he had never worked at a school. He had been hired by the school district as a psychological assessment consultant. He was a good looking, fast talking, well-educated man who spoke the language of education that was quite prevalent at the time. He had convinced the district administration that he had to answers to what alternative education needed. The second week of school, he called the staff of our school together and announced, "I worked through the summer and I will be taking my two week vacation starting Monday, going to Maui. See you when I get back." We were, of course, surprised but handled the situation quite easily. I believe it was at that time that Owen and I made the decision that no matter who the principal was, this was our school. Over the two weeks that the principal was away, we established the standards that we decided were best and the students rapidly fell in line. When he returned, the school continued to perform extremely successfully. It was confirmed what we believed, that the students were, in general, seeking an atmosphere in which they could become successful. Rigorous expectations equaled a smooth-running school. The principal really didn't make much difference, it was the minute to minute, day to day interaction between the students and the teachers that really counted. On the other hand, when the principal returned, we began to observe his true worth. In the area of computers, he was truly ahead of his time. By whatever means, he was able to locate the money necessary to purchase seven Radio Shack-80 desktop computers. For a school with an enrollment of forty students, this was an outstanding accomplishment. Our local high school was limited to 25 computers, located in the library where teachers had to schedule time during which they could take their class across campus to utilize them. Our students, many of whom already had computers in their homes, took to them immediately. Owen was able to plug his math students directly into programs that addressed a great deal of remedial math topics. I was able to put my students studying English into programs that helped with grammar and spelling drills. The system was all set to go except there was one problem. Owen and I had no background in computers, at all. The principal spent a lot of time trying to help us become comfortable with this new field. This helped but truthfully, our students were far more successful in showing us how to operate a computer. Once we got the hang of it, computers became an extremely useful tool.

The remainder of the school year went well. There were times when the principal, due to his lack of experience dealing with student discipline, struggled. This made our jobs as classroom teachers sometimes more difficult because we often felt that there was a lack of support from the principal. But by the end of the school year, Owen and I were fairly satisfied that things were going the way we liked them. The students were attending regularly and were being successful academically. We had seven students graduate during the year and everyone was looking forward to summer break and the next school year. It never seemed like the principal was destined to spend a lot of time at our school. Like most school principals, he was a successful politician. Sure enough, by the beginning of the next school year, he was gone, moved into the district office as Assistant Superintendent. After a few years in that job, he was hired to work at the Superintendent of County Schools Office. After several years there, he became the County Superintendent of Schools, the top job in county education. He succeeded there as well and eventually was hired at another county school district in Northern California. I saw him a few years later. He seemed happy.

THE BONGO WOMAN

Her name was Jamie. She was tall and when I first saw her, frightfully thin. Her dad had been one of the legends of Fillmore High School athletes. When the basketball season began her Freshman year, her dad came to me and offered to coach the Junior Varsity team. My immediate concern was that although she was tall enough to play Varsity, I didn't know whether her long, thin arms and legs could withstand the rough, physical play that the older girls could sometime give out. I therefore consented to have her stay on the JV team. She turned out to be much stronger and tougher that I had initially thought. She dominated the other players that she competed against that first year. By her Sophomore season, I felt confident that she was truly something special. For the next three seasons she was our leading scorer. The name Bongo Woman came from one of her teammates who said the manner in which she ran down the court looked and sounded like she was playing the bongos with her feet. She finished her career as the leading scorer in Fillmore High School's Girls Basketball history. She was named Tri-Valley League Player of the Year, All Ventura County and All C.I.F. Southern Section. After high school she attended and graduated from The U.S. Army Academy at West Point, New York. She played basketball there and served her time in The Army quite successfully. After completing her tour of duty, she married and together she and her husband opened a training facility for military personnel that prepared individuals for serving in the Middle East. The training center taught languages and local customs to the attendees. They also offered these services to business corporations who were sending employees to that area of the world. She and her husband were extremely successful financially and established world wide reputations. My concerns about her fragility were proven incorrect.

SISTER AURORA

Just after Christmas in 1977 I heard from an old high school friend that there was a teaching position at an elementary school in West Los Angeles. The previous eighth grade teacher had resigned at the end of the first semester so I applied for the position and was interviewed by the principal, Sister Aurora. The school was located just West of the 405 Freeway in an area that combined several commercial buildings and some middle-class homes and apartments. I was hired and excited to be working in my first full-time classroom experience. The class that year consisted of only sixteen students, two Anglos, two African-American and eight Mexican-American. There were eight girls and eight boys. The job was made more difficult because the previous teacher had not been a strong personality. The students had taken advantage of this situation and made it difficult to get them to accept my more demanding expectations. Sister was getting a lot for a little in hiring me. For the momentous sum of $610.00 per month, I had many assignments. I was responsible for teaching English, History, Science and Government. The Principal, Sister Aurora came into the classroom each day after lunch to teach Math and Religion. During that time, I was the P.E. teacher for all the classes from Kindergarten to Eighth Grade. A P.E. teacher for the younger students meant teaching them a few exercises and then perhaps a few skills such as catching a ball. Tossing a ball to a six-year-old and then watching the ball bounce off their face a few times was always funny.

Having attended a Catholic high school myself, I had forgotten about an old habit. I am not referring to the outfits worn by the sisters. The tradition was, and probably still is, that when an adult entered the classroom, every student jumped to their feet. On the third day that I was working, Sister Aurora quickly and quietly came into the classroom as I was writing on the chalkboard. I was startled when all sixteen of my students flew in unison out of their desks and came to attention beside their desks. All of my old memories from my school days at Santa Clara suddenly returned.

Sister Aurora was a great mentor for me that first year as a full-time teacher. She had high standards for everyone under her supervision, staff and students. As a first-year teacher, she was concerned about my abilities. At the beginning of each month she required that I meet with her to lay-out my teaching lesson plans. It took me awhile to develop this skill and expectations. By the end of the semester, I had been able to win over most of the eighth-grade students and it was exciting and gratifying to watch them leave the school and move on to high school. As my second school year approached, I met with Sister a few days to prepare for the upcoming year. My teaching assignments continued to be the same and she wanted me to expand the after school athletic program. It was simple to attract the students to play a sport and Sister located the extra coaches (mostly parents) and provided the money for uniforms and equipment. I was able to put together a second flag football team for the sixth-grade boys and the school's first girl volleyball team. During the Winter season, I developed a fifth and sixth-grade boy's basketball team. In the Spring, I was able to put together a girl's softball team and a track and field team for boys and girls. All of this experience was helpful to me over the rest of my teaching/coaching career as I was responsible to selecting equipment, scheduling games for all of the teams, setting-up and taking down equipment for home games and transporting the athletes all over the Los Angeles area. One time, Sister directed me to select some trophies that would be awarded to the students at our annual end of year sports banquet. After I did so, I presented sister with the bill from the trophy company. When she looked at it, she frowned a little and said, "Well, we will see." When the trophies arrived a few days later, I noticed that the trophy company had reduced the price by about thirty percent. Another example of the power of the habit. The annual sports banquet was always an outstanding affair. The parents attended and contributed food in a pot-luck dinner for everyone and two football players from U.C.L.A. joined us and made nice speeches. The students were always made to feel special.

The second year that I taught at the elementary school in West Los Angeles was quite different from the first. My class that year was twice the size of the first school year. The emotional make-up was much less mature that the previous class. The class contained several immature members who made it difficult to conduct instruction involving the entire group. Two young Hispanic girls worked extremely hard to achieve a grade of A in every subject. Another characteristic of both girls was that their religion meant a great deal to them. It seemed like either of them would have been interested in entering a convent. Eighth grade students can come in wide variety of body types. Boys are either tall, gangly fellows extremely uncomfortable with their bodies or at the opposite end, they could be small, fragile little guys who could never fit into the mainstream of the class. With the girls, it was that they either developed physically much faster than average or they were years behind showing their age. In both cases, the girls were far more interested in members of the opposite sex than most of the boys ever were. Within this class of thirty-three students, there was a broad spectrum.

One of my female students was involved in the Police Cadet Program at the local L.A.P.D. Station. Several students from the community would meet on Saturdays to participate in training about police activities. This included both physical exercise as well as classroom instruction about police work. She really enjoyed the program so one afternoon, she asked me if the class could take a walking field trip to have a tour of the Police Station and holding cells. I thought that it might be a good civics lesson and Sister gave permission. My student began to assemble the paperwork and most of the students were excited about going. As the date approached, about eight of the students had not returned the parental permission slips so as the students were dismissed to go to lunch, I kept the eight in the classroom to encourage the return of the signed slips. The student who was organizing the trip stayed in the room and we were both shocked to hear that the eight students who had not co-operated did not want to go on the field trip, they said that their parents were refusing to allow them to attend the trip. When I asked why, the students all said that because they were in the country illegally, they and their parents were concerned that they would be exposed and forced to return to Mexico. I was ashamed that I had not even considered such a scenario. At this point, Sister decided to just cancel the entire trip. I always felt bad about the students missing such an opportunity and that the "illegal" students were embarrassed.

Near the end of the school year, Sister had given permission for a field trip to the beach. This was for members of the class who wanted to participate. One afternoon, the students were discussing plans about what they wanted to do as far as food and activities. Most were excited and joined in the talk enthusiastically. I was surprised that a couple of boys were not involved so I asked what they would like to do. Both boys said they didn't want to go at all because, "the white girls just wanted to walk around with their asses sticking out". This caused a huge explosion and I had to terminate the planning session. We eventually took the trip with about seven or eight boys choosing to not attend. They spent the day at school with Sister in a classroom.

KING TUT

One afternoon, Sister came into the classroom and announced that she had been able to obtain permission for the sixth, seventh and eighth grade classes to attend the King Tut Exhibit to be held at the Los Angeles County Museum of Art. She had arranged for three buses to transport us along with the three teachers, some parent chaperons and herself. The staff at our school spent a couple of weeks preparing the students (and ourselves) for what we would be seeing at the museum. I must admit, the students were very excited and on the day of our visit, they conducted themselves quite well. The exhibit was extremely large, covering several rooms at the museum. Many times a field trip can be filled with potential problems but this event came off smoothly and the students really seemed to enjoy everything about it.

SMOOTH

His name was Jose Zavala and from the day he enrolled at our school, he was a pain in the ass. He wasn't a kid who cause confrontations and he didn't actually disrupt the calm in the classroom but by his second week he had managed to upset everyone, students and staff alike. He had a way of putting people down with a hate filled comment or two that just added up exponentially. He was particularly rude to the female students, commenting on their clothing and appearance. That always had the effect of causing the girls to lash out at him. He was often equally rude to the guys in the classroom and several times I was forced to intervene to prevent a fight. It became obvious to everyone that he was an extremely sad and lonely person. One afternoon, after one of his typical unacceptable remarks directed at one of the girls, I said, "Jose, you are really smooth with the ladies". That got a big laugh from everyone and interestingly, Jose seemed to calm down after that. The name stuck and after that day, everyone called him Smooth. Over the next couple of months, he seemed to offer up fewer and fewer rude comments to anyone. It seemed like he was beginning to be more comfortable at our school and realized that he didn't need to attract as much attention with his negativity. One morning I arrived at school and was told by the principal that

Jose had been involved in an auto accident. He was riding in a car in Bardsdale (a community across the river from Fillmore) with some other young people that not finished high school, they were never my students. It was extremely dark and foggy that night and the driver of the car was going way too fast. The car left the roadway and crashed into an orange tree. Jose was killed instantly and the other passengers survived but were badly injured. Interestingly, the students in our school were not as upset as they had been about the previous loss of young people's lives. They were relatively quiet but seemed to return to normal much more quickly.

THE PIRUVIANS

There is a small community east of Fillmore called Piru. It is an unincorporated town that has a long history in the county. The is no middle school or high school there so the students attend Fillmore schools after sixth grade. Over the years that I taught at the alternative high school, several students came to our school from Piru. Without exception, the personal characteristics of these students were almost exactly the same. They were all fun loving kids who were interesting to talk to and interact with but as far as interest in academics, it just made no sense for them. Having fun was all that life was about. An example was Lorenzo. We had taken a group of students on a field trip and a couple of students including Lorenzo lived in Piru so they asked to be dropped off at their home instead of riding the bus to Fillmore where they would have to find a ride back to their houses. This was a regular occurrence whenever we passed through Piru so the bus driver agreed. Four students got off the bus and Lorenzo was among them. The other three walked out of the bus and proceeded down the street to their homes. Lorenzo was so excited to be home that he ran off the bus and then up the street, cut in front of the bus and then back across the street and down an alley. He reminded me of an overly exuberant dog being let out of a car after a long trip. The kids from Piru were just a little different.

CONCLUSION

When I chose to train for and become a teacher, I based the decision on personal experience. Several members of my family had been teachers, including my mother. It seemed like a good choice for a career. The hours seemed attractive, the school day lasted until early afternoon, there was no weekend work and in those days, teachers had three months off each summer. I found out quickly that the work-day lasted much farther into the evenings with papers and working on lesson plans. When I decided to include coaching, that meant a couple of hours work after the school day and the idea of weekends off quickly disappeared. Coaching at the high school level also meant time put into summer practices and games. The concept of having three months off each summer also dried up about seven years into my career. State and local governing bodies decided that the students needed to be in class earlier and earlier in order to help them prepare for college and the post high school years in their careers. When I made my career choice, I had never heard of the concept of "non-student days". They were the worst. Teachers were required to work, attending district wide workshops that were meant to enhance our teaching skills. It always seemed like a wasted day listening to some expert telling us that we needed to change everything we had been doing because they had a better way of reaching kids. Looking back over my thirty-four year career, it now seems so clear to me that the reason I became a teacher was to provide an opportunity for the students to succeed. I believe that I did that. Since retiring, many people have asked me if I missed teaching. I have always responded, "I don't miss the bureaucracy and government interference. I do miss the students. Their enthusiasm keeps you going day after day."

www.ingramcontent.com/pod-product-compliance
Lightning Source LLC
Chambersburg PA
CBHW021429070526
44577CB00001B/136